this is my faith

Buddhism

Tick Tock

by Holly Wallace

An Hachette UK Company
www.hachette.co.uk

This edition published 2012 for Index Books Ltd by TickTock, a division of Octopus Publishing Group Ltd,
Endeavour House, 189 Shaftesbury Avenue, London, WC2H 8JY.
www.octopusbooks.co.uk

ISBN 978 1 84898 699 2

A CIP catalogue record for this book is available from the British Library

Printed in Singapore
10 9 8 7 6 5 4 3 2 1

Picture credits
t = top, b = bottom, c = centre, l = left, r = right,
OFC = outside front cover, OBC = outside back cover

Corbis: 5b, 11, 16, 17t, 17b, 19c, 20, 25b, 27t, 27b, 28. Getty: 15c. Plan UK and Plan International: OFC, 1, 2, 4b, 5t,
6all, 7all, 10t, 12t, 14t, 15b, 18all, 20t, 21all, 22t, 24t, 26all, 27c, 31t, OBC. Shutterstock: 19b, 25t. Superstock: 29t, 29b.
World Religions PL/ Christine Osborne: 23, 24. World Religions PL/ Nick Dawson: 13, 15t, 19t, 22, 25c.

Every effort has been made to trace the copyright holders, and we apologize in advance for any unintentional omissions.
We would be pleased to insert the appropriate acknowledgments in any subsequent edition of this publication.

Contents

Words that appear in **bold** are explained in the glossary.

I am a Buddhist

"My name is Yuranan and I am 14 years old. I live in a village in Chiangrai in northern Thailand. My family follow the religion of **Buddhism.** We are **Buddhists.**"

"There are three main groups of Buddhists. We are **Theravada** Buddhists. Theravada means 'way of the elders'. The other groups are **Mahayana** Buddhists, Mahayana means 'the great way', and **Vajrayana** Buddhists. Vajrayana means 'the diamond way.'"

As a Buddhist Yuranan tries to be good and kind and caring towards other people.

Most Buddhist homes have a statue of Siddattha Gotama, the greatest teacher of Buddhism.

"Buddhists do not believe in God. We follow the teachings of Siddattha Gotama. He was a man who lived in India 2,500 years ago. He became known as **the Buddha.**"

"The Buddha means someone who has gained **Enlightenment.** This means being able to see things as they really are."

Buddhists use the lotus flower as a symbol of Enlightenment.

This is a temple for Theravada monks.

"Buddhists can pray any-where but often we will go to a **temple.** Buddhist temples are very beautiful."

My family

"I live with my family. I have a father and mother and two younger brothers. My father works in a nearby village. He is always busy."

"I respect my parents and will do whatever they tell me to do. The Buddha taught that we should show respect to all people."

This is Yuranan with some members of his family.

6

Yuranan helps his mother to prepare the family meals and to look after his younger brothers.

"We believe in trying to do good things and to look after other people. I help my parents by doing jobs at home."

"In our home we have a **shrine** with a picture of the Buddha. We kneel before the shrine every day."

The image of Buddha reminds people of his teachings and of his kindness and peacefulness.

Yuranan's family gives food to a Buddhist monk. He takes it back to the temple to share with the other monks.

"My family gives food and money to the monks from the temple. The monks do not own very much apart from their robes."

LEARN MORE: What is Buddhism?

- Buddhism began in India where Siddattha Gotama or the Buddha was born. After the Buddha died, Buddhist monks travelled to other countries telling people about the Buddha's teachings.

Thailand
Bangkok

- Today there are about 400 million Buddhists living all over the world.

WORLD MAP

Britain
EUROPE

USA

South K

Nepal

India Myanmar

Sri Lanka

Indonesia

- There are many Buddhists and Buddhist temples in Europe, the USA and Britain.

- In countries such as Thailand and Sri Lanka, most people are Buddhists. Yuranan also has relatives in Myanmar.

- Buddhists do not worship the Buddha as a god but they respect him as a very special person who has shown them the way to Enlightenment.

Mahayana Buddhists worship special beings called bodhisattvas. Buddhists pray to them and ask them for help and guidance in their lives.

The Buddha gained Enlightenment as he sat and **meditated**. Meditation is a very important part of Buddhist practice. It means clearing and calming the mind so that it becomes restful and peaceful.

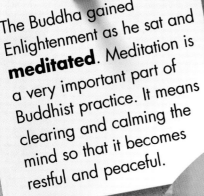

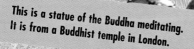

This is a statue of the Buddha meditating. It is from a Buddhist temple in London.

What I believe

"Buddhists try to follow the teachings of the Buddha. We also try to avoid doing harm to any living thing in everything we do. We are taught to be kind to people, even if we are in a bad mood."

"In our daily lives, we try to follow the Three Jewels of Buddhism. We call them jewels because they are so precious."

Many Buddhists try to visit the temple every day. Here a woman places a piece of gold leaf on a statue of the Buddha as a sign of love and respect.

Buddhist monks sit in front of a huge statue of the Buddha in the Wat Bowon monastery in Thailand.

"The first jewel is the Buddha himself.
The second jewel is the **Dhamma**, the Buddha's
teachings. The third jewel is the Sangha.
The Sangha means the Buddhist monks, nuns and
everyone who has made Buddhism the most important thing in their lives."

The Story of the Buddha

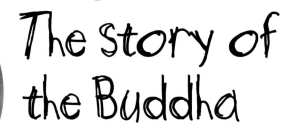

"Siddattha Gotama was an Indian prince. He was born in a place called Lumbini, in the country we now call Nepal. A wise man told his father that Siddattha would become a great king or teacher."

"Before he became the Buddha, Siddattha was married and had a son."

Siddattha was rich and powerful and lived a life of luxury. But he gave this up to discover the meaning of true happiness.

The story of how Siddattha became the Buddha.

"One day, Siddattha saw an old man, a sick man and people crying at a funeral. He had never seen old age, illness or death before and had never seen so much unhappiness. Then he saw a holy man who had given up all his possessions but was very happy."

Siddattha gained Enlightenment as he sat under a Bodhi tree. After this he was known as the Buddha.

"Siddattha decided to leave home and become a wandering holy man. He travelled far and wide looking for the answer to unhappiness. One day he sat down under a tree to meditate. There he gained Enlightenment. He understood why people are unhappy and how their unhappiness could be stopped."

The Buddha's teachings

"The Buddha taught us that the reasons why people suffer and are not happy is because they are greedy and selfish. People keep wanting things that they do not have."

"As Buddhists we try to live in a different way so that we can leave our greed and selfishness behind."

In the area where Yuranan lives there are many statues of the Buddha. These help to remind Buddhists of his teachings.

In Buddhism, a wheel with eight spokes is often used as a symbol for the Buddha's teachings.

"The way the Buddha taught us to live is called the **Noble Eightfold Path.** It says we should think, act and speak kindly, and also treat people well and with care."

"We also make five promises: not to harm any living thing; not to steal; not to be greedy; not to lie and not to drink alcohol or use drugs."

Many monks look after animals in their temples including cats and sometimes even young deer.

Giving food to the monks is a type of Dana, which means 'giving'. This is a way to follow the Buddha's teachings and show care for others.

"Buddhists believe that, when you die, you are born again into another life. This can happen again and again until you may finally reach **Nirvana.**"

15

LEARN MORE: Our special books

- There are lots of special books in Buddhism. Different groups of Buddhists have their own **sacred** books.

Puppets were often used to tell stories from the Jataka tales. Puppets were used because actors thought it was not respectful to play the part of the Buddha.

- The most popular book for Theravada Buddhists is the Dhammapada. It is made up of over 400 verses which are the sayings of the Buddha.

- The Dhammapada helps us to understand the Buddha's teachings and offers advice and guidance. Buddhists treasure this text and try to live by it.

- The Jataka tales are part of the Dhammapada. They are stories about the Buddha's past lives. Each story has a special message.

- The Hae'in-sa temple in South Korea has one of the world's oldest complete collections of Buddhist scriptures in the world.

The Buddha's teachings were often spread by people singing and playing instruments.

- The Jataka tales help us to understand the Buddha's teachings on sharing, helping others, living wisely and being a good friend.

This is a drawing showing a chariot racing across the sky. It is a scene from one of the Jataka stories.

How I worship

"I go to worship in a temple near to my home. There is no special day for worship. Sometimes I go with the rest of my family. But I can drop in on my way to or from school."

Yuranan and some of his family worship together at their local temple.

Each offering has a special meaning. Fresh flowers wilt and die, a reminder that nothing lasts for ever.

"In the shrine room of the temple, there is a statue of the Buddha. We leave offerings of candles, flowers and **incense.**"

"Candles light up a room just as the Buddha's teaching lights up people's lives and shows them the way to live."

Candles are left in front of the shrines for people to light when they visit the temple.

Buddhists can meditate at home or go to a local temple or just find somewhere quiet.

"Many Buddhists like to meditate every morning to start their day. Some meditate on their own; others do it in a group."

Monks and nuns

"The Buddha spent most of his life living as a monk. Some Buddhists also choose to leave their homes and families and live as monks and nuns."

"There are many more monks than nuns. They spend their lives meditating, reading the sacred books and helping people to understand the Buddha's teaching."

Girls and women of all ages can become Buddhist nuns.

These young boys are called Samanera or 'novice monks'.

"In Theravada Buddhist countries, such as Thailand, boys often spend a few months or years living as monks so that they can learn more about Buddhism."

"Boys join a monastery when they are teenagers. They have lessons for several hours a day and an hour of **chanting**."

The novice monks collect food, serve the meals and tidy up afterwards.

After offering the monks food, many Buddhists ask for help or advice from their local monks.

"Many monks work as teachers or help people in the local community in other ways. They also help people to understand more about Buddhism."

Wesak

"For me and my family, the most important festival in the year is when we remember the Buddha's birth and Enlightenment. We believe that these things happened on the same day, but in different years and during a full moon. This festival is called Wesak. It happens in May or June."

"We hang flowers and streamers around the house. All the statues of the Buddha are washed and shiny. We also send cards to our family and friends."

Buddhists in different parts of the world celebrate Wesak, or Buddha Day, in their own special way. These monks in Nepal wear colourful costumes as part of the festival.

Some Buddhists wash the statues of the Buddha before they celebrate Wesak. Here volunteers in Thailand are washing the statues in the street. They will then decorate them with flowers and garlands.

"We visit the temple and take offerings
for the Buddha. Then we pour scented water
over the image of the Buddha. At night,
the statue of the Buddha is taken outside.
We walk around it carrying candles or lamps.
This reminds us of how the Buddha's teaching
lights up our lives."

Other festivals

"**Loy Krathong** is a special festival in Thailand. It is the festival of the floating boats and takes place on the night of the full moon in November."

"Our boats are called krathongs. We make them from palm leaves or paper and they contain a candle, flowers and incense. In the evening, we take them to the water. As they float away, so all bad luck is supposed to disappear".

People in Thailand make a wish as they set their boats on the water. If the candle stays burning until the boat floats out of sight, their wish will come true.

Sometimes the older children take water pistols and buckets of water to spray over people. It is thought the water washes away bad luck.

"In Thailand we celebrate the New Year, or Songkran, in April. We sprinkle scented water over the monks and our elders to show respect."

"Each year in February, some Buddhists celebrate Nirvana Day. This is when we remember the death, or passing into Nirvana, of the Buddha."

Buddhists celebrate Nirvana Day by meditating or visiting Buddhist temples or monasteries.

The temple elephant carries the Buddha's sacred tooth through the streets on the last day of the festival.

"In the city of Kandy, in Sri Lanka, they celebrate Perahera. This is also known as the festival of the Buddha's Sacred Tooth."

Special occasions

"There are many special times in a Buddhist's life. For me, my special time will be when I join the temple during the summer holidays."

"When I join the temple I will have my head shaved and wear a robe, and live a simple life like the other monks for a few weeks."

Many young Buddhist boys spend a few weeks as novice monks in their local temple. They are given robes and a food bowl and help collect food for the older monks.

The young boys are dressed up in colourful clothes and headdresses. They are treated like princes for three days before they join the monastery as novice monks.

"The Poi Sang Long is a ceremony which takes place in Thailand. It celebrates young boys joining the Mae Hong Son monastery as novice monks."

"When a baby is born, its parents may take the child to the temple to be blessed by the monks. Sometimes the monks visit the baby at home."

Children are taught to honour and respect the Buddha as soon as they are old enough.

A Buddhist funeral procession. Buddhists are usually cremated and never buried. Their ashes are either buried or kept in a temple.

"When someone dies we believe they are born again into a new life. This is called **rein-carnation**. This may happen many times. By following the Buddha's teachings, people may be reborn closer to Nirvana."

LEARN MORE: *Holy places*

- For most Buddhists the holiest places are in India and Nepal. These are the places where the Buddha gained Enlightenment, gave his first teaching and died.

- Where the Buddha was born in Lumbini in Nepal, there is a square pool. Buddhists believe his mother bathed here just before giving birth to her son.

- The monks in this photo are worshipping under a bodhi tree in Bodh Gaya, India. The tree grows in the spot where the Buddha was Enlightened.

Prayer flags have been left in the branches of the bodhi tree. Prayer flags are pieces of cloth with symbols or words on them which send out good wishes on the wind.

This sacred building is at Sarnath near Varanasi in India.

- This building, or stupa, is said to have been built on the exact spot where the Buddha gave his first talk about his beliefs. The holy men who listened to him became his first followers.

- The holiest shrine for Buddhists is the Mahabodhi Temple in Bodh Gaya, India. This was built thousands of years ago on the spot where the Buddha was Enlightened. The bodhi tree (left) grows next to the temple.

The Mahabodhi Temple has a pyramid-shaped tower that is 50 metres tall. Inside is a large statue of the Buddha. The statue faces exactly towards the spot where the Buddha was Enlightened.

Glossary

Buddhist nuns

Bodhisattvas Special beings worshipped by Mahayana Buddhists. Bodhisattva means 'Enlightened beings'.

Bodhi tree A large type of fig tree. Buddhists believe that the Buddha gained Enlightenment while sitting under this type of tree.

The Buddha The title given to a man called Siddattha Gotama. It means the one who has gained Enlightenment.

Buddhism The religion of the people called Buddhists.

Buddhists People who follow the teaching of the Buddha.

Chanting Speaking or singing words or sounds in rhythm. In Buddhism, chanting is a way to prepare for meditation.

Cremated When a dead person's body is burned.

Dhamma The Truth, or the teachings of the Buddha.

Enlightenment Realising the true meaning of life. Buddhists sometimes describe this as waking up from a deep sleep.

Incense Sticks of sweet-smelling spices that are burnt for their smell.

Loy Krathong The festival of the floating boats in Thailand. At this time some Buddhists also remember the holy footprint of the Buddha on the beach of the Namada River in India.

Mahayana One of the three main groups of Buddhists. This group believes in the importance of kindness and understanding as well as wisdom.

Meditate To sit quietly and clear your mind so that you feel calm and relaxed.

Monks Men who give up their homes and belongings to follow a religious way of life. The Buddha himself lived as a monk.

Nirvana Perfect peace and happiness that is reached by people who are Enlightened.

Noble Eightfold Path According to the Buddha's teachings, this is the way to find the answer to what causes suffering and unhappiness and how to bring t hem to an end. His 'path' helps followers to stop wanting things that they do not need and to stop holding on to wrong ideas.

Buddhist monks

Novice Someone who is new or inexperienced in something. A novice monk is someone who is training to become a monk.

Nuns Women who give up their homes and belongings to follow a religious way of life.

Reincarnation Being born into a different body when you die.

Sacred Another word for holy.

Shrine A place that has an image of the Buddha.

Stupa A holy shrine or building built over what are thought to be relics of the Buddha or over copies of his teachings.

Symbol An object or sign that has a special meaning and that stands for something else.

Temple Where Buddhists go to pray and worship. All temples contain a large image or a statue of the Buddha.

Theravada One of the main groups of Buddhists. This type of Buddhism is found in Sri Lanka.

Vajrayana One of the three main groups of Buddhists. This group developed in India about 1,500 years ago.

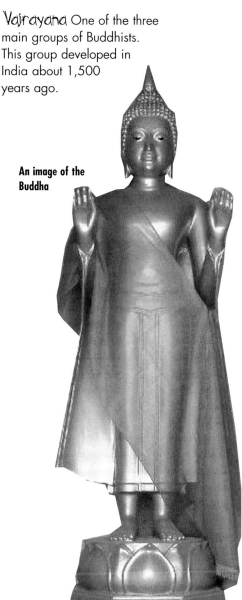

An image of the Buddha

Index